T0014178

Allosaurus/Alosaurio

By Joanne Mattern
Illustrations by Jeffrey Mangiat

Reading Consultant: Susan Nations, M.Ed.,
author/literacy coach/consultant in literacy development
Science Consultant: Darla Zelenitsky, Ph.D.,
Assistant Professor of Dinosaur Paleontology at the University of Calgary, Canada

WEEKLY READER®
PUBLISHING

Please visit our web site at www.garethstevens.com.
For a free color catalog describing our list of high-quality books,
call 1-800-542-2595 (USA) or 1-800-387-3178 (Canada).
Our fax: 1-877-542-2596

Library of Congress Cataloging-in-Publication Data

Mattern, Joanne, 1963–
  [Alosaurio. Spanish & English]
  Allosaurus / by Joanne Mattern ; illustrations by Jeffrey Mangiat /
Alosaurio / por Joanne Mattern ; ilustraciones de Jeffrey Mangiat.
      p. cm. — (Let's read about dinosaurs dinosaurs / Conozcamos a los dinosaurios)
    Includes bibliographical references and index.
    ISBN-10: 0-8368-9422-7   ISBN-13: 978-0-8368-9422-6 (lib. bdg.)
    ISBN-10: 0-8368-9426-X   ISBN-13: 978-0-8368-9426-4 (softcover)
    1. Allosaurus—Juvenile literature. I. Mangiat, Jeffrey, ill. II. Title.
III. Alosaurio.
  QE862.S3M331918   2009
  567.912—dc22   2008042952

This edition first published in 2009 by
Weekly Reader® Books
An Imprint of Gareth Stevens Publishing
1 Reader's Digest Road
Pleasantville, NY 10570-7000 USA

Copyright © 2009 by Gareth Stevens, Inc.

Executive Managing Editor: Lisa M. Herrington
Creative Director: Lisa Donovan
Senior Editor: Barbara Bakowski
Art Director: Ken Crossland
Publisher: Keith Garton
Translation: Tatiana Acosta and Guillermo Gutiérrez

All rights reserved. No part of this book may be reproduced, stored in a retrieval system,
or transmitted in any form or by any means, electronic, mechanical, photocopying,
recording, or otherwise, without the prior written permission of the copyright holder.
For permission, contact **permissions@gspub.com**.

Printed in the United States of America

1 2 3 4 5 6 7 8 9 10 09 08

Table of Contents

- - - - - - - - - - - - -

Contenido

Boldface words appear in the glossary./
Las palabras en **negrita** aparecen en el glosario.

A Different Lizard

Meet Allosaurus (al-loh-SAWR-us). Allosaurus was a big dinosaur. It lived in North America.

- - - - - - - - - - - - - - -

Un lagarto diferente

Conozcan al alosaurio. El alosaurio era un dinosaurio muy grande. Vivía en América del Norte.

Allosaurus was about as long as three small cars. It was as tall as an elephant.

— — — — — — — — — — — — — —

El alosaurio era casi tan largo como tres autos pequeños. Era tan alto como un elefante.

Allosaurus's name means "different lizard." Its back bones were different from the bones of other known dinosaurs.

- - - - - - - - - - - - - -

"Alosaurio" significa "lagarto diferente". Los huesos de su espina dorsal eran distintos a los de otros dinosaurios que se conocían.

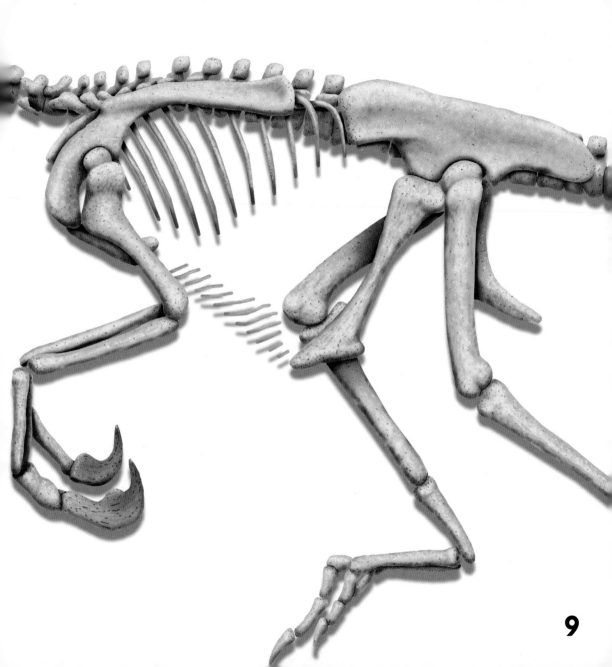

9

Allosaurus had short arms and a long, heavy tail. It ran on long back legs.

El alosaurio tenía brazos cortos y una cola larga y pesada. Corría sobre sus largas patas traseras.

tail/
cola

arms/
brazos

legs/
patas

11

Claws and Jaws

Allosaurus had three fingers on each arm. Each finger had a long, sharp claw.

- - - - - - - - - - - - - -

Garras y mandíbulas

El alosaurio tenía tres dedos en cada brazo. En cada dedo tenía una garra larga y afilada.

claws/
garras

Allosaurus ate meat. It hunted other dinosaurs. Allosaurus used its long claws to grab **prey**.

— — — — — — — — — — — — — —

El alosaurio comía carne. Atacaba a otros dinosaurios. Para atrapar a sus **presas**, el alosaurio usaba sus largas garras.

15

Allosaurus had strong jaws with long, sharp teeth. The teeth curved backward. They were just right for ripping into prey.

- - - - - - - - - - - - - - -

El alosaurio tenía una mandíbula fuerte con largos y afilados dientes. Los dientes se curvaban hacia atrás. Eran ideales para desgarrar a las presas.

A Peek at the Past

Scientists found the first Allosaurus **skeleton** about 130 years ago. They have found many Allosaurus bones in western North America.

- - - - - - - - - - - - - -

Un vistazo al pasado

Los científicos encontraron el primer **esqueleto** de alosaurio hace unos 130 años. Desde entonces han hallado muchos huesos de alosaurio en el oeste de América del Norte.

Montana/
Montana

South Dakota/
Dakota del Sur

Wyoming/
Wyoming

Utah/
Utah

Colorado/
Colorado

UNITED STATES/
ESTADOS UNIDOS

New Mexico/
Nuevo México

Oklahoma/
Oklahoma

North/
Norte

West/
Oeste

East/
Este

South/
Sur

KEY/CLAVE

= Allosaurus lived here/Zonas
donde vivían alosaurios

19

Allosaurus died out long ago. Today, we can see its skeleton in **museums**. Skeletons help us learn about Allosaurus and its world.

Los alosaurios desaparecieron hace mucho tiempo. Hoy en día, podemos ver su esqueleto en los **museos**. Los esqueletos nos ayudan a conocer mejor a los alosaurios y el mundo en que vivían.

ALLOSAURUS

21

Glossary/Glosario

museums: places where people can see interesting objects on display

prey: animals that are hunted and eaten by other animals

skeleton: the bones that make up an animal's body

- - - - - - - - - - - - - - -

esqueleto: los huesos que forman el cuerpo de un animal

museos: lugares donde la gente puede ver exhibiciones de objetos interesantes

presas: animales que son atacados y devorados por otros animales

For More Information/Más información

Books/Libros

Alosaurio/Allosaurus. Pebble Plus Bilingual (series). Helen Frost (Capstone Press, 2007)

Descubriendo dinosaurios con un cazador de fósiles/Discovering Dinosaurs With a Fossil Hunter. I Like Science! Bilingual (series). Judith Williams (Enslow Publishers, 2008)

Web Sites/Páginas web

Dinosaurs for Kids: Allosaurus/Dinosaurios para niños: Alosaurio
www.kidsdinos.com/dinosaurs-for-children.php?dinosaur=Allosaurus
This site has fun facts, illustrations, a map, and a time line./
Esta página presenta datos entretenidos, ilustraciones, un mapa
y una línea cronológica.

Zoom Dinosaurs: Allosaurus/Enfoque en los dinosaurios: Alosaurio
www.enchantedlearning.com/subjects/dinosaurs/dinos/Allosaurus
Find facts, pictures, maps, and printouts of Allosaurus./Encuentren datos,
ilustraciones, mapas e información para imprimir sobre los alosaurios.

Publisher's note to educators and parents: Our editors have carefully reviewed these web sites to ensure that they are suitable for children. Many web sites change frequently, however, and we cannot guarantee that a site's future contents will continue to meet our high standards of quality and educational value. Be advised that children should be closely supervised whenever they access the Internet.

- - - - - - - - - - - - - - - - -

Nota de la editorial a los padres y educadores: Nuestros editores han revisado con cuidado las páginas web para asegurarse de que son apropiadas para niños. Sin embargo, muchas páginas web cambian con frecuencia, y no podemos garantizar que sus contenidos futuros sigan conservando nuestros elevados estándares de calidad y de interés educativo. Tengan en cuenta que los niños deben ser supervisados atentamente siempre que accedan a Internet.

Index/Índice

About the Author

Joanne Mattern has written more than 250 books for children. She has written about weird animals, sports, world cities, dinosaurs, and many other subjects. Joanne also works in her local library. She lives in New York state with her husband, four children, and assorted pets.

Información sobre la autora

Joanne Mattern ha escrito más de 250 libros para niños. Ha escrito textos sobre animales extraños, deportes, ciudades del mundo, dinosaurios y muchos otros temas. Además, Joanne trabaja en la biblioteca de su comunidad. Vive en el estado de Nueva York con su esposo, sus cuatro hijos y varias mascotas.